Introduction

The colors are fabulous, the clay is soft, and you buy some and take it home. Now what? Good question! This book is your answer!

I have spent years developing projects and working with over 1,000 students to create fun and easy polymer clay projects. I continue to teach clay art classes weekly. Whether you are a beginner or you are looking for new ideas, there is something here for everyone at any skill level.

This book is designed to be easy to use, and includes lots of pictures of the clay projects in progress for you to follow. I hope it will inspire you to pick up a lump of clay and see where it takes you. The characters in this book can be embellished by adding your own special touches. Do you think the mama duck needs a hat or the ducklings should have bows on their heads? Maybe they should be an entirely different color. It is all up to you; have fun creating!

Visit my studio online at www.TerryTaylorStudio.com and see what else you can do with polymer clay! I have used polymer clay to illustrate many picture books for children, and my artwork is published regularly in children's magazines and children's educational products.

Project Difficulty

The projects in this book are grouped by difficulty in each section. Projects with one star are the easiest to do, and are good for beginners. Two star projects are a little more difficult, and three star projects are the most complicated and have more steps. All of the projects in this book have been tested with students and are kid-approved for maximum fun.

Tools and Supplies

Did you know that anything can be a clay tool? The projects in this book were designed to use only a small number of tools, most of which you will have around the house.

Let's gather your tools so you are all prepared for the upcoming projects. You will need wooden chopsticks, straws, clay tool for cutting, pencil, paperclips, roller or dowel, wooden craft sticks, pasty cutter with ruffle edge, scissors, CD, aluminum foil, and wax paper. You will also need a flat baking pan to use when you bake your projects in the oven.

Safety Tip!
Once a tool has been used for clay it is best not to use it for food. Keep it only for clay use.

All of the projects in this book were made with polymer clay. Polymer clay is a plastic based clay. It is especially good for young artists because it is soft and easy to work in your hands. Polymer clay comes in a full range of colors available at craft stores and online art supply stores. It usually is sold in 2 ounce (57g) bricks which is more than enough for any project in this book. Store unused clay in plastic zip bags. Polymer clay remains soft until baked, even if it is exposed to the air.

Money Saving Tip!

You can mix polymer clay to make new colors. If you need a different color you don't have, try mixing to make it!

Basic Techniques

1. **Work Surface:** Use a piece of wax paper on a hard flat surface. Wax paper will keep your piece from sticking to the table and make turning it easier. Be careful when working on wood as the clay can stain the surface. When working with children, I have found that a plastic table cloth is helpful to keep the mess under control.

2. **Keeping Colors Clean:** Washing your hands between clay colors will help keep the colors clean and keep them from mixing with bits of clay left on your hands. I also rub a little hand cream on my hands before working to keep the clay from sticking to my hands.

3. **Conditioning the Clay:** The first step before making any polymer clay project is conditioning the clay. Soften the polymer clay in your hands by rolling it into a ball and then squeezing it in your fingers; repeat the process until the clay is not crumbly and forms a ball without cracking. When you are able to roll a ball and flatten it with no cracks, the clay is ready to make a project. Skipping this step can cause your finished projects to crack, not stick securely together, or fall apart when baking. If the clay is really crumbly, mix one or two drops of mineral oil into the clay to help soften it up.

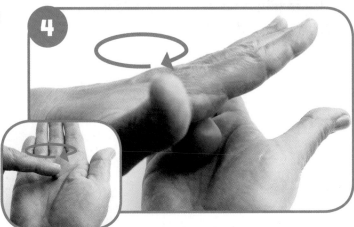

4. **Making a Ball:** Roll the clay in a circular motion in the palm of your hands to form a ball for basic building of characters. For smaller-eye sized balls, use a finger tip to roll the ball in the palm of your hand.

5. **Making a Cone Shape:** Make a ball of clay and then place it on your work surface and with one or two fingers roll one side of the ball to form a point.

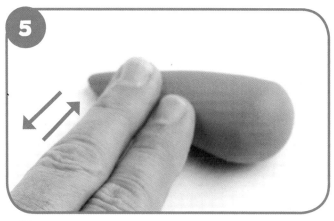

6. **Rolling Long Coils:** To make a coil from the clay, start by rolling the clay into a ball. Place the ball on the table and roll gently back and forth with one hand in one direction to form a tube shape. When the clay is long enough, use both hands to lengthen the coil. While you are rolling back and forth move your hands outward. The more you roll the clay, the longer and thinner it will be. It is important to not put too much pressure on the clay as you are rolling it—that will flatten the coil.

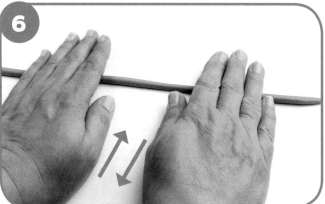

7. **Making Short Fat Coils:** Start by making a ball of clay, and then roll it back and forth in one direction. Stop rolling when the clay looks like the picture.

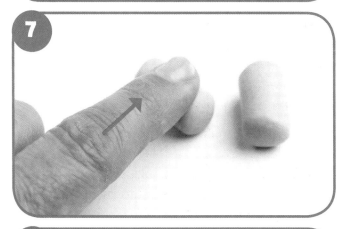

8. **Making Sheets or Slabs of Clay:** Flatten conditioned clay on wax paper with a roller or wooden dowel against a hard surface. There are also polymer clay acrylic rollers and clay conditioning machines available from art supply stores and online.

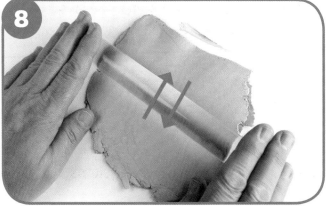

Basic Techniques

9. **Cutting the Clay:** It is best to use a clay tool with a narrow edge for cutting clay. Polymer clay is soft and is easily cut with a paperclip or dull knife. Once you have used a kitchen utensil for clay you should not use it for food again. Using a straight edge like a craft stick will help you get a nice clean straight cut. For fancy cuts, try a pastry cutter to get a ruffled edge.

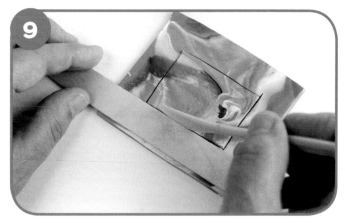

10. **Support while Baking:** Propping up the clay that is raised during baking will keep the sculpture from sagging or flattening out. Use a ball of aluminum foil to support any raised or vertical surface. If you have an open box, stuff the inside with balled up wax paper while baking to help the box keep its shape. Aluminum foil and wax paper used to support a piece can be used over and over again, so keep it handy.

11. **Using a Template:** Trace or copy the templates from the book, and cut out the shape with scissors. Place the template on flattened clay. Cut along the edge of the shape with a clay tool.

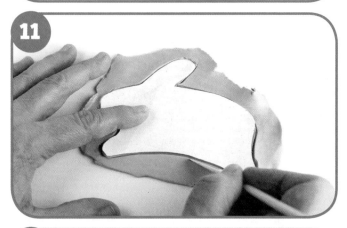

12. **Making "Magic" Color Coils:** Take some mixed-up different color clay, roll it in your hands until clay is smooth and the surface has no cracks. Then follow the rolling coils steps. After you have a good length of coil, hold one end of the coil still with your hand and roll the other end away from you to make the clay colors spiral around the coil. When one side is twisted to your liking, hold the other end and repeat the process until the whole coil is has twisted colors. It is important to not put too much pressure on the clay as you are rolling it—that will flatten the coil.

Hold Clay

Tips for getting the most out of your "Magic" color clay

Start with this.

End with this.

Condition It!
How do you know your "magic" color clay is ready to make a project? Roll the "Magic" color clay in your hands until the clay is soft and smooth and the surface has no cracks.

Roll it.

Fold it.

Make a twist.

"Magic" Coils!
To get even thin stripes of color around your coils, fold it two or three times while rolling. Folding the coil will distribute the colors evenly for the length of the coil.

"Magic" Color!
Be careful not to mix your "Magic" color clay too much or you will have a muddy mess. Mix just enough so that the clay stays together and the colors are bright.

Ornaments, Signs & Dangles

Make cute ornaments for your holiday tree or brighten up your walls with festive dangles. Decorate your door with a bright personalized bedroom sign. Create your own unique pizza or cupcake "flavor" that is tasty looking!

Making the high relief sculpture projects in this section will build your basic clay working skills. So grab some clay and let's go!

Penguin Pal
Difficulty Level: ★

Materials

2 oz. brick of blue clay
¾ inch ball of red clay
½ inch ball of white clay
¾ inch ball of yellow clay
white & black clay for eyes
Tools: paperclip

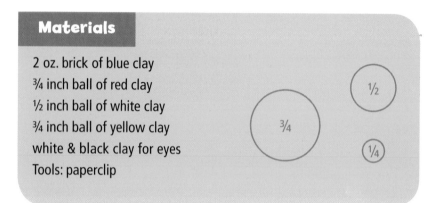

Directions:

1. Start with blue clay. Divide the clay into 4 quarters. Roll 2 quarters of the clay into a ball and shape into a short, fat coil for the penguin body. Place the body on a piece of wax paper.

2. Set aside a ¼ inch ball of white clay to use for eyes. Roll remaining white clay into a ball and flatten with a roller to make an oval. Place white oval in the middle of the penguin body and press gently to attach. Roll 1 quarter of the blue clay into a ball to form the head. Position head over white oval, and press to attach to the body.

3. Divide remaining blue clay into two equal parts, and roll each part into cones to form wings. Position wings on opposite sides of the body with the pointed ends down. Press wings firmly onto each side of the body to attach.

4. Set aside a ¼ inch ball of yellow clay to use for beak. Divide the remaining yellow clay in half, and roll into two balls. Position the balls under the penguin and press toward body to flatten slightly and attach. Use the paperclip to add detail lines to each foot.

5. Add two small white balls for eyes; press gently to secure. Add two small balls of black clay for pupils of eyes, and press gently in place.

6. For the beak, roll a small yellow cone of clay. Position between the eyes on the face. Open one end of the paperclip and use the point to add nostril holes in beak.

7. Divide red clay in half. Roll one part into a fat coil, and flatten. Position on head and press to attach. Divide remaining red clay into two parts. Roll a coil and a ball.

8. Put the ball on the top of the hat for a pom-pom. Add the coil around the bottom of the hat. Use the side of the paperclip to add texture to the brim and pom-pom.

Press closed paperclip into the back of the head leaving some of the clip sticking out to loop the ribbon through for hanging. (See picture at right.)

Ask an adult to bake your finished project on a wax paper lined cookie sheet according to clay manufacturer instructions on the package.

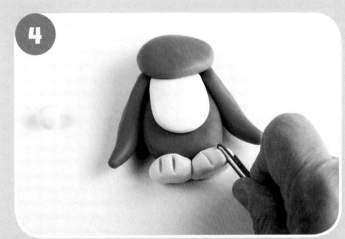

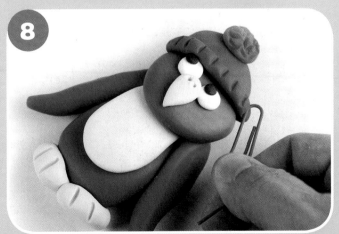

Snowman Ornament
Difficulty Level: ★

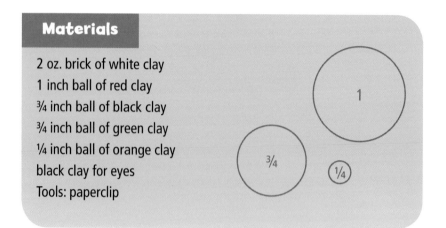

Materials

2 oz. brick of white clay
1 inch ball of red clay
¾ inch ball of black clay
¾ inch ball of green clay
¼ inch ball of orange clay
black clay for eyes
Tools: paperclip

1

¾

¼

Directions:

1. Divide the white clay into three balls, one small, one medium, and one large.

2. To form the snowman, place the large ball on a piece of wax paper; flatten slightly with the palm of your hand. Overlap the medium size ball on top of the large ball. Press firmly with the palm of your hand to join the pieces. Repeat process with the small ball for the head.

3. Add two small black balls for eyes; press in place. Add three small black balls for buttons; press in place as shown. For the carrot nose, roll a ball of orange clay and form a cone shape by lightly rolling one side of ball to make it come to a point, and add lines using the side of the paper clip. Press the rounded end of the paper clip into the white clay under the "carrot" to form the smiling mouth.

4. To make the scarf, roll a coil of red clay about 5 inches long and a coil of green clay the same size. Place coils next to each other and twist together; roll to form the scarf. Drape around neck and down the side of the snowman. Press in place to secure. Save remaining twisted coil to use for the bow on the present and the hatband.

5. Take half of the black clay, roll into a ball, and flatten slightly. Pick up and tap edges of circle on a flat surface to flatten sides and form a square.

6. Roll a coil of black clay for the hat brim, and press to secure. Add a hatband with a small coil of the twisted clay.

7. To form the gift, roll a ball of red clay the same size as the hat. Flatten slightly, pick up and tap edges of circle on a flat surface to flatten sides and form a square shape.

8. Create bow from twisted coil, by forming two loops. Add coil down middle of package.

   Press closed paperclip into the back of the head leaving some of the clip sticking out to loop the ribbon through for hanging.

   Ask an adult to bake your finished project on a wax paper lined cookie sheet according to clay manufacturer instructions on the package.

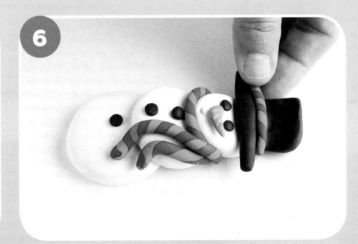

Tasty Cupcake
Difficulty Level: ★ ★

Materials

(½) 2 oz. brick of brown clay
½ inch ball of pink clay
½ inch ball of purple clay
¼ inch ball of white clay
Tools: craft stick, clay tool, chopstick, roller

½

¼

Directions:

1. Roll the brown clay into a fat coil. Place on a piece of wax paper, and flatten coil slightly with your palm; keep the coil slightly rounded.

2. Flatten the purple clay with a roller. Using a clay tool, cut a curve wider than the brown clay.

3. Place the flattened clay over the brown clay, curved piece up. Cut off extra clay on the sides and bottom, wrap purple clay over the edge of the brown clay to form a smooth edge.

4. Add vertical indents to purple cupcake wrapper using the edge of the craft stick.

5. Press the end of a chopstick into the edge of the purple cupcake wrapper to create a ruffled look.

6. Roll pink clay into a long coil about 12 inches long. Keep the diameter of the coil as consistent as possible.

7. Place the pink coil across the brown clay, leaving a little of the brown clay showing between the cupcake wrapper and the frosting coil. Extend coil past the edge of the brown clay and loop back next to previous coil to form the first layer. Loop the coil back and forth to make about 7 rows decreasing the width each time to form the frosting. At the end of the 7th loop break off the remaining clay and roll end to a point. Curl point to make the top of the cupcake.

8. Roll very thin coils of white and purple clay. Cut coil to make sprinkles, and place on frosting at angles; press gently to attach.

Press paper clip into back before baking to form hanging loop or attach a magnet to the back after baking.

Ask an adult to bake your finished project on a wax paper lined cookie sheet according to clay manufacturer instructions on the package.

Sweet Cakes!
What flavor cupcake and icing do you like? Get creative!

Grab your favorite color clays and "cook up" your own tasty-looking treat!

Pizza Deluxe
Difficulty Level : ★ ★

Materials

(½) 2 oz. brick of tan clay
(¼) 2 oz. brick of of light yellow clay
½ inch ball of red clay
½ inch ball of green clay
¼ inch ball of dark brown clay
Tools: roller, clay tool, scissors, pencil, paper

½

¼

Directions:

1. Place tan clay on wax paper, and flatten with a roller. Trace the template below on a piece of paper and cut it out with scissors, use the template to cut the pizza shape. Set aside the extra tan clay.

2. Roll remaining tan clay into a coil and place on the wide end of the slice to form the edge of the crust. Press gently to flatten and attach. Cut off any extra clay.

3. Roll a thin coil of red clay and position next to pizza crust. Flatten with fingers and make the edge look irregular like spread sauce. Trim off extra clay and save to use for pepperoni.

4. Flatten the light yellow clay with a roller. Position to slightly overlap the red clay. Cut off any extra yellow clay at the edge of the pizza shape. Flatten with fingers and make it look irregular and "melty."

5. Roll out green clay and cut into rectangles to make green peppers.

6. Make a ball of tan clay ½ inch in diameter, flatten, and cut circle of clay in half to form mushroom caps. Make a coil from the remaining tan clay and flatten to form the mushroom stems. Roll a thin coil of dark brown clay; position and attach under the mushroom caps. Use clay tool to rough up the edge.

7. Make a ball of red clay and flatten to form the pepperoni; speckle with white clay by putting a little bit on the end of a chopstick and pressing into the red clay. After adding white, flatten gently with roller to smooth out.

8. Position all toppings on pizza and press gently to attach.

Ask an adult to bake your finished project on a wax paper lined cookie sheet according to clay manufacturer instructions on the package.

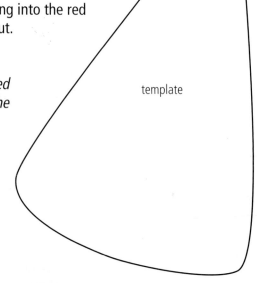

template

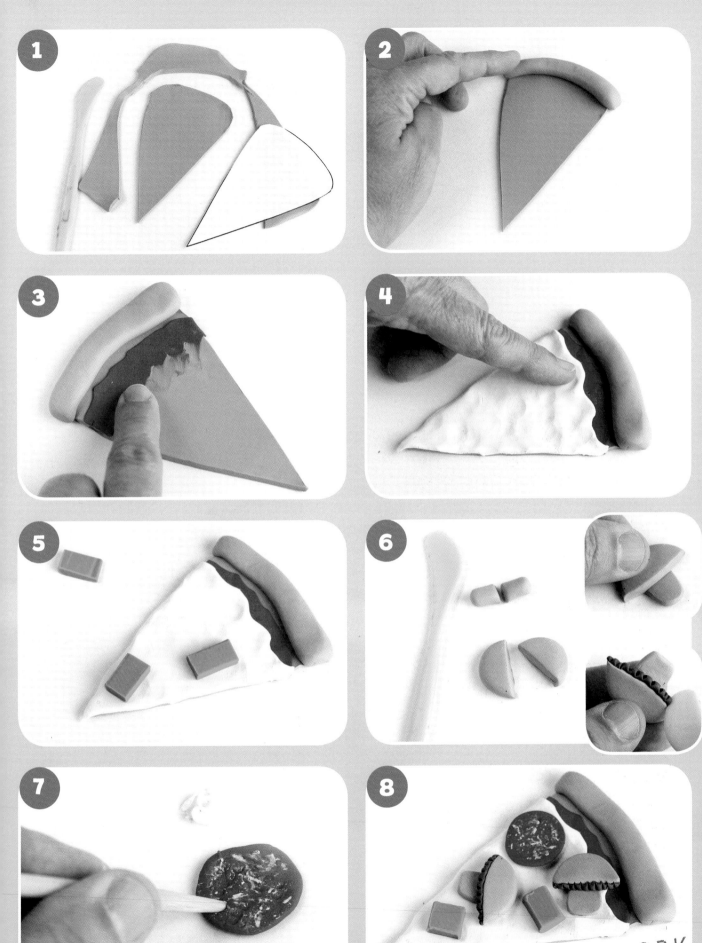

Bunny Bedroom Sign

Difficulty Level : ★ ★

Materials

(½) 2 oz. brick of green clay
(¼) 2 oz. brick of of blue clay
½ inch ball of white clay
½ inch ball of yellow clay
¾ inch ball of pink clay
white & black clay for eyes
Tools: roller, clay tool, straw, paperclip, craft stick, scissors, pencil, paper

½

¾

Directions:

1. Flatten light blue clay with a roller; trace and cut out the template below to make bunny-shaped clay. Place template on clay and cut along edge with clay tool. Smooth edges of bunny with your finger.

2. Roll a ½ inch ball of white clay, and press onto the tail of the bunny; press gently to attach. Add texture using the craft stick.

3. Roll a small white ball and a smaller black ball for the eye of the bunny. Add a small pink ball for the nose and a small pink coil to the ear. Position and press all pieces gently to attach.

4. Add whiskers, eyebrow, and feet details with the side of the paperclip. Open the end of the paperclip to add three dots by the nose.

5. Flatten green clay with a roller. Position completed bunny in the middle of the green clay. Use the craft stick for a straight edge. Cut a rectangle around the bunny using the clay tool. Smooth edges and round corners of green clay with your fingers.

6. Use the side of the paperclip to add grass texture to the green clay.

7. Use a straw to punch a hole on either side of the green rectangle. After piece is baked, string a ribbon through holes to hang.

8. Roll a coil of clay and spell out your name on the bunny. Space out all the letters before you press to attach.

   Ask an adult to bake your finished project on a wax paper lined cookie sheet according to clay manufacturer instructions on the package.

Make it Match!

Make your bedroom sign match your room.

Use the basic ideas in this project to create your unique bedroom sign. Have fun!

template

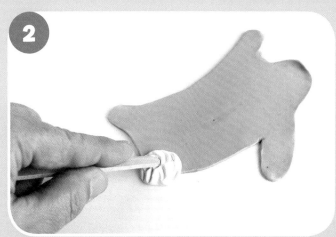

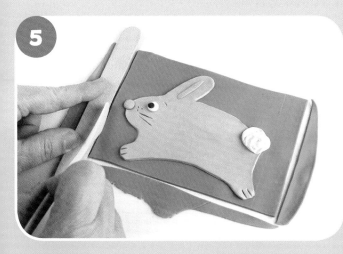

Elephant Bedroom Sign

Difficulty Level : ★ ★

Materials

(½) 2 oz. brick of green clay
(½) 2 oz. brick of blue clay
(½) 2 oz. brick of magenta clay
1 inch ball of yellow clay
white, black & pink clay for details
Tools: roller, clay tool, paperclip, pastry cutter, scissors, pencil, paper, straw

1

Directions:

1. Flatten magenta clay with a roller; trace and cut out the template below to make elephant-shaped clay. Place template on clay and cut along edge with clay tool. Smooth edges of elephant with your finger.

2. Roll a ball and flatten to form the ear. Position the ear on the elephant, and press gently to attach. Roll a small coil of the magneta clay to make the tail of the elephant. Position and press gently to attach. Add a small black ball to the end of the tail, and add texture to end of tail using the side of the paperclip.

3. Roll a small white ball and a smaller black ball for the eye of the elephant. Roll a small pink ball for the end of the trunk. Press all pieces gently to attach.

4. Add detail lines to the trunk, mouth, ear and feet using the paperclip.

5. Flatten blue clay and green clay with a roller to the thickness of a piece of cardboard. Cut one edge of the green clay with a pastry cutter to create a zig zag edge. Overlay the green clay on the blue, leaving half the blue showing. Press to attach. (Do not use pastry cutter for food once it has been used for clay.)

6. Position completed elephant in the middle of the green and blue clay. Cut a rectangle around the elephant using a pastry cutter.

7. Roll a small ball of yellow for the sun and some coils to make the rays. Using a straw, punch out a hole on either side of the rectangle. Add grass texture to the green clay by using the edge of the paperclip.

8. Roll a coil of yellow clay and spell out your name on the elephant. Press each letter gently to bond.

   Ask an adult to bake your finished project on a wax paper lined cookie sheet according to clay manufacturer instructions on the package.

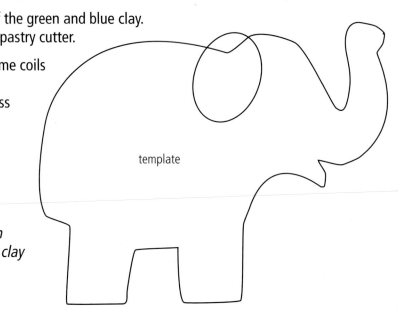

template

Sweet Treats Dangle
Difficulty Level : ★ ★ ★

Materials

(½) 2 oz. brick of blue clay
two 1 inch balls of purple clay
two 1 inch balls and ¼ inch ball of brown clay
two ¾ inch balls and ½ inch ball of red clay
1 inch ball of white clay
1 inch ball of pink clay
¾ inch ball of green clay
Tools: paperclip, computer disk, clay tool, straw

Sundae Directions:

1. Roll three balls of clay 1 inch in diameter, one purple, one brown, and one pink. Place the purple ball on wax paper and flatten slightly with palm of your hand; flatten the brown and pink balls the same way.

2. Overlap the flattened balls and press gently to attach. Set aside.

3. Flatten the blue clay with the roller. Use a computer disk for a template and cut half a circle to make the bowl shape.

4. Cut a smaller half circle about two inches wide to form the base of the bowl. Roll unused blue clay into a coil to use for the rim of the bowl.

5. Overlap the three flattened balls with the blue half circle of clay and press gently to attach. Place the 2" blue half circle of clay under the bowl and press gently to attach.

6. Add texture to all three scoops of ice cream using a craft stick. Place the blue coil around the top edge of the dish. Press to attach, and cut off extra clay.

7. Roll a coil of white clay. Place over the ice cream as shown. Loop the coil back and forth about 7 times, decreasing the width each time to form the whipped cream. Curl point to make the top of the whipped cream.

8. Add sprinkles, red dots and the strawberry to the sundae. Strawberry directions are on page 30.

Embed a paper clip into back before baking to form hanging loop, and make a hole in the base of the dish with a straw.

Ask an adult to bake your finished project on a wax paper lined cookie sheet according to clay manufacturer instructions on the package.

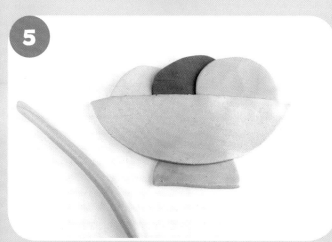

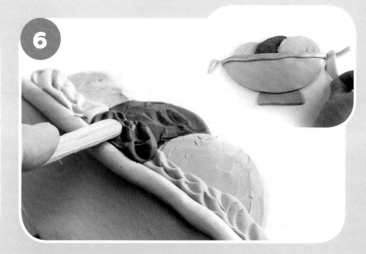

Ice Cream Cone Directions:

1. Roll three 1 inch balls of clay, one pink, one purple, and one brown. Roll one ½ inch ball of red clay.

2. Place the pink ball on the wax paper and flatten with roller; flatten the purple ball the same way. Cut off the bottom of each circle, and roll into separate coils.

3. Overlap the flattened balls and press gently to attach. Roll the brown clay into a cone shape.

4. Flatten the brown cone shape with roller. Make the sides of the triangle straight by tapping the edges on the table to smooth.

5. Add a crisscross pattern to the cone by gently pressing a craft stick into the clay. Angle the craft stick diagonally to form a diamond pattern.

6. Place the ice cream cone under the purple clay and press gently to attach. Add coils to the base of each scoop.

7. Use a craft stick to sculpt the coil to look like ice cream that just came off a scoop. Repeat for the second scoop.

8. Add small balls of red clay for berries. Press gently to attach.

   Embed a paper clip into back before baking to form hanging loop. Use a straw to make a hole in the bottom of the cone.

   Ask an adult to bake your finished project on a wax paper lined cookie sheet according to clay manufacturer instructions on the package.

Delicious Delights!
Ice Cream comes in about a zillion flavors!

Grab your favorite "flavored" clays and invent your own dream ice cream!

Add some different colors to make chocolate chips, marshmallows, or berries!

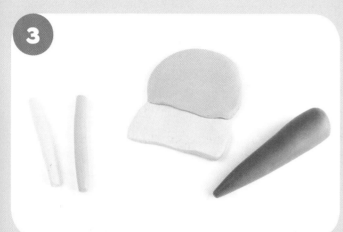

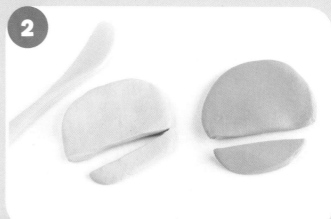

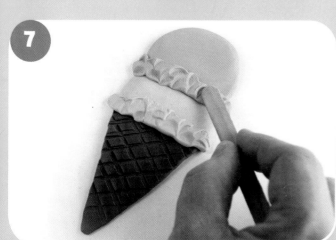

Strawberry Directions:

1. Use a ½ inch ball of red clay, roll into a slight cone shape.

2. Use end of paperclip to add strawberry seed markings on the entire surface.

3. Flatten a ½ inch ball of green clay with roller. Trace the template below to cut out the strawberry leaves. Place the leaves on the top of the strawberry, and press gently to attach. Use paperclip to add details.

   Embed a small paper clip into the top before baking to form a hanging loop.

   Ask an adult to bake your finished project on a wax paper lined cookie sheet according to clay manufacturer instructions on the package.

Template

Dangle Stringing Directions:

Start with Individual pieces that are baked and cooled.

4. Cut a 8-inch length of ribbon to loop through the sundae paperclip loop. Fold ribbon in half and knot.

5. Cut 18 inches of ribbon, and tie one end through the hole in the base of the dish. Optional: Add a bow under the dish, if desired, by tying a 5-inch piece or ribbon through the hole and forming a bow.

6. Thread ribbon through the paperclip loop in the ice cream; tie to secure at two inches from the base of the sundae dish. Run the ribbon down the back of the ice cream cone, and poke a loop of ribbon though the hole in the cone. Thread remaining ribbon through the loop.

7. Tie strawberry to the end; add a bow above the berry and cut off extra ribbon.

Ribbons Galore!
Craft ribbon comes in a wide variety of colors and patterns. Pick a complementary color to go with your dangle!

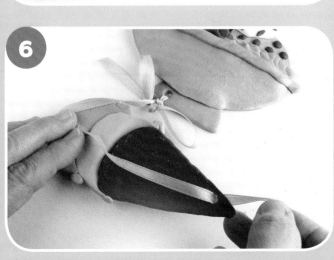

Garden Bugs Dangle

Difficulty Level : ★ ★ ★

Butterfly Directions:

1. Roll four 1 inch balls of pink clay. Place a pink ball on wax paper, and flatten with roller and fingers to form an oval shape; flatten the remaining three balls the same way.

2. Arrange and overlap the flattened shapes to form the base of the wings, and press gently in center to attach.

3. Roll a ½ inch ball of black clay into a coil to form the body of the butterfly. Roll a ¼ inch ball of black clay for the head of the butterfly. Position the body and head between the wings, and press to attach.

4. Roll two balls of each color, yellow, green, blue, and purple; each ball should be about ¼ inch in diameter. Add to wings in a symmetrical fashion. Press to flatten and attach.

5. Press a V-shaped 2-inch piece of black craft wire into the head of the butterfly. Smooth clay over hole. Divide the last ¼ inch ball of black clay in half, and add one small ball of black clay on the end of each antenna.

6. Use the edge of the paperclip to add texture all around the wing edges, and body.

   Embed a paper clip into back before baking to form hanging loop, and punch a hole in one lower wing with the straw.

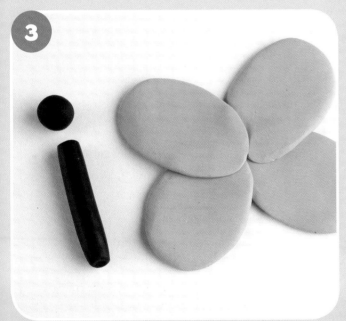

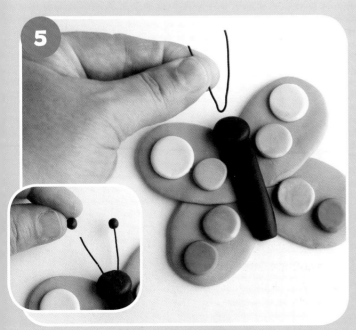

Ladybug Directions:

1. Make a ball of red clay about 1 inch in diameter. Place the clay on wax paper, and flatten slightly with the palm of your hand. Keep the top rounded. Roll the black clay into a ball ½ inch in diameter for the head. Press to attach to the body.

2. Make a line down the middle of the back using the side of a paperclip.

3. Roll four ¼ inch balls of black clay, and attach two on either side of the back. Press a V-shaped 2-inch piece of black craft wire into the head of the ladybug. Smooth clay over hole.

4. Divide the last ¼ inch ball of black clay in half, and add one small ball of black clay on the end of each antenna.

   Embed a small paper clip into back before baking to form hanging loop.

Bee Directions:

5. Roll the yellow clay into a ball about 1 inch in diameter. Place the clay on wax paper, and flatten slightly with the palm of your hand. Keep the top rounded. Roll the black clay into a ball ½ inch in diameter for the head. Press to attach to the body.

6. Make a thin coil of black clay, spiral around the yellow ball, and press gently to attach.

7. Take the two ½ inch balls of white clay; flatten with roller. Position the white clay next to each other and press the bee body in the middle. Add lines on each wing with the side of the paperclip.

8. Use a ¼ inch ball of black clay to make a cone, position on the tail of the bee, and press gently to attach. Press a V-shaped 2-inch piece of black craft wire into the head of the bee. Smooth clay over hole. Divide the last ¼ inch ball of black clay in half, and add one small ball of black clay on the end of each antenna.

   Embed a small paper clip into the back before baking to form hanging loop.

Go Buggy!
Use the directions and skills you have learned creating the bugs in this project to create new bugs!

Leaves and Flower Directions:

1. Start with two ½ balls and one ¾ ball of green clay. Roll the white clay into five balls ½ inch in diameter, and make one ball of yellow clay ½ inch in diameter.

2. Roll each green ball of clay into a cone shape. Place the green clay on wax paper, and flatten with roller to form the three leaves.

3. Use the side of the paperclip to make vein markings on the front surface of the leaf. Make a hole in the wide end of each small leaf using a straw.

4. Working on wax paper, position the five white balls to form a circle with an opening in the middle. Indent and flatten each ball with your finger to form petals of the flower. Place the yellow ball of clay in the middle and flatten to form the center of the flower. Use the side of the paperclip to indent each petal.

5. Position the flower at the wide end of the big leaf and press to attach. Use the open end of the paperclip to add dots to the middle of the flower.

    Embed a small paper clip into the back before baking to form hanging loop.

    Ask an adult to bake your finished project on a wax paper lined cookie sheet according to clay manufacturer instructions on the package.

Dangle Stringing Directions:

Start with individual pieces that are baked and completely cooled.

6. Cut 8-inch length of ribbon to use as a hanging loop and thread through the paper clip in the butterfly. Fold the ribbon in half and knot the end. Cut 18 inches of ribbon and thread through the hole in the butterfly; knot the end.

7. Thread ribbon though the hole one of the small leaves. Position and tie ladybug below leaf.

8. Thread ribbon though the hole in the next small leaf. Position and tie bee below the leaf. Secure the leaf with the flower on the end, and tie a bow above the flower. Cut off extra ribbon.

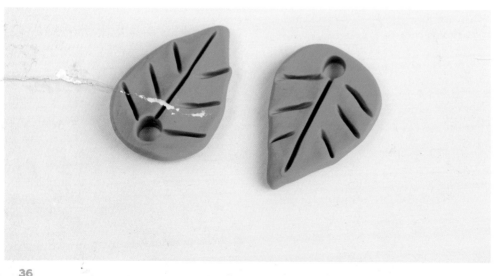

Sculpture Pals

Owls, alligators, and kitties, oh my! Now that you have learned some clay working skills, it is time to move to the next level, freestanding sculptures! Make some of these cute critters to liven up your space. Or give them as special gifts to your family and friends.

Let's get 3D together! As you are making the projects in this section, give them your own personal touches by posing them to give them some character. Get creative and make these critters truly unique!

Duck & Ducklings

Difficulty Level: ★

Materials

Mama Duck: 1½ inch ball; ¾ inch ball of white clay
two ½ inch balls of white clay
two ½ inch balls of orange clay
½ inch ball of yellow clay

Ducklings:
two 1 inch, two ¾ inch, and two ½ inch balls of yellow clay
six ½ inch balls of orange clay
white & black clay for eyes on all ducks
Tools: paperclip

Directions:

1. To make the mama duck, start by rolling balls of clay 1½ inch and ¾ inch, and two ½ inch cones of white clay. Next roll two ½ inch balls of orange clay, then roll one ½ inch ball of yellow clay. Roll small balls of black and white for eyes.

2. To form the body of the mama duck, roll the 1½ inch ball into a slight coil shape by rolling back and forth in one direction. Place one white ball on one end of the coil to form the head. Press firmly to attach to the body. Pinch the opposite end of the coil to form tail feathers.

3. Take the two white cone shapes; flatten slightly to form the wings. Position wings on either side of the body, and press gently to attach.

4. Add feather texture using the end of the paperclip on the wing and the rest of the duck.

5. To make the feet, take the orange clay balls; flatten and pinch one end of each to form the feet. Center the feet under the duck, and press the body gently onto feet to attach. Add detail to feet with edge of paperclip.

6. Flatten the remaining ball of yellow clay, and tap one edge on the table to form the base of the beak. Center on head, wrap around either side of the head, and press to attach. Add nostril holes with the end of the paperclip.

7. Add two small white and black balls for the eyes, and press to attach. Add eyebrows with the rounded end of the paperclip.

8. For the the ducklings, make two 1 inch, two ¾ inch, and two ½ inch balls of yellow clay. Then make six ½ inch balls of orange clay. Roll small balls of black and white for eyes.

To make the ducklings repeat steps 1-7.

Ask an adult to bake your finished project on a wax paper lined cookie sheet according to clay manufacturer instructions on the package.

Just Duckie!
To make a cute note holder just embed a paperclip in the duck's back before baking.

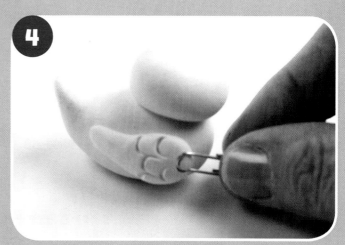

Laughing Lizard

Difficulty Level: ★

Materials

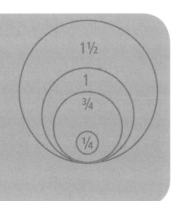

1½ inch ball of purple clay
four ¾ inch balls of purple clay
1 inch ball of green clay
¼ inch ball of pink clay
white & black clay for eyes
Tool: paperclip, foil

Directions:

1. Divide your clay and roll into balls.

2. To make the lizard's body, roll the largest ball of purple clay into a cone shape. To create this shape, first start by making a thick coil, then continue rolling with your hand on half of the coil. The end will start to thin out and become pointed. Continue rolling until the lizard body is about 8 inches long.

3. Roll the four ¾ inch balls back and forth in one direction to make short coils for the feet.

4. Position feet under the body as shown. Press feet firmly toward the body to attach.
   Flatten the front of the feet with your thumb.

5. Roll the green clay into a coil slightly shorter than the length of the lizard body. Attach the coil down the middle of the lizard's back.

6. Add eyes by making two small balls of white clay and two smaller balls of black clay to form each eye. Position on the head as shown, and press gently to attach.

7. Form the lizards mouth by slicing halfway through the larger end of the coil with a clay tool. Rock the tool up and down to create the mouth.

8. Roll the pink clay into a coil and flatten. Add tongue to the bottom jaw and press gently to attach. (Continued on page 44.)

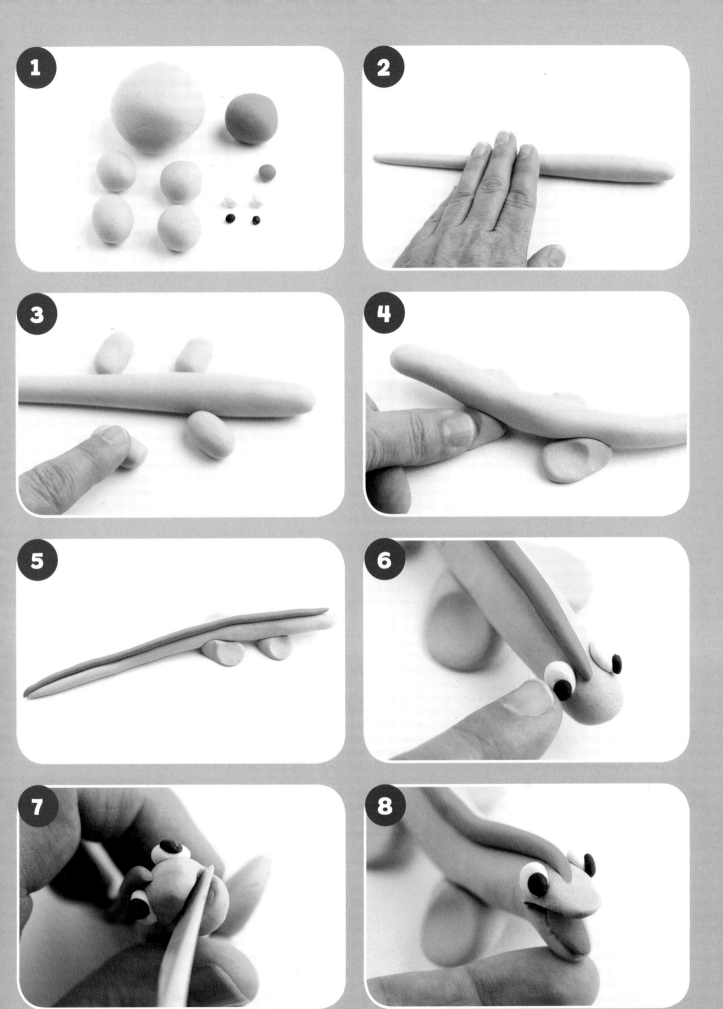

Directions continued:

9. Use the side of a paper clip to add detail lines to feet.

10. Open one end of the paperclip and add dots to create texture on both the sides, tail and the feet of the lizard.

11. The flat edge of the paperclip is used to create detail on the back ridge.

12. Use the end of the paperclip to make two nostrils.

13. Use paperclip to indent the middle of the tongue.

14. Position body and tail to give the lizard some personality.

15. Use a ball of foil under the head to support it and keep it in position while baking. Remove foil only after lizard is completely cooled.

Ask an adult to bake your finished project on a wax paper lined cookie sheet according to clay manufacturer instructions on the package.

Leaping Rainbow Lizards!

Use your favorite color clay to make your lizard any color combination you like. Add scale texture to your lizard by using the rounded end of the paperclip.

Try using some "Magic" color clay for the back ridge to give your lizard a unique look.

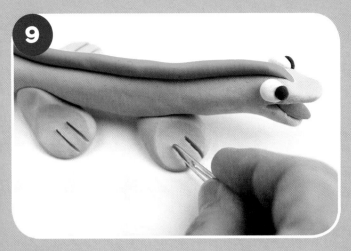

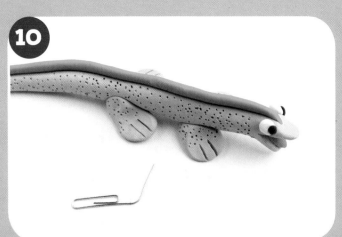

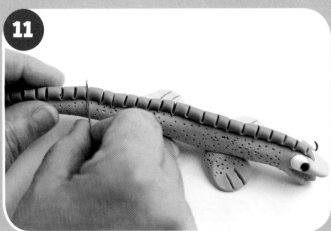

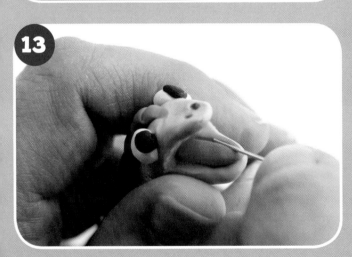

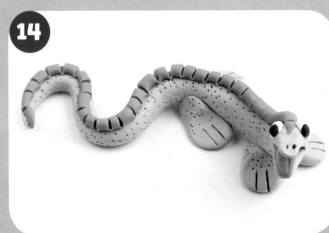

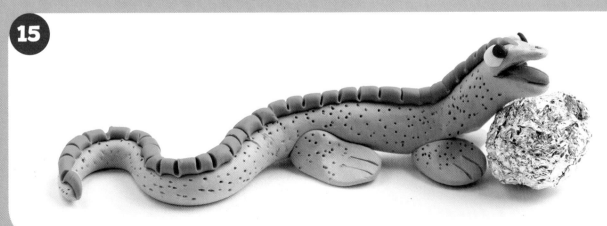

Hoot Owl
Difficulty Level: ★ ★

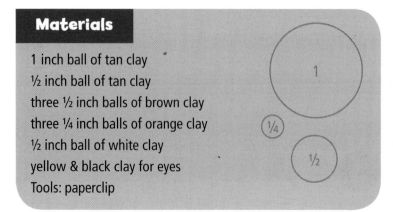

Materials

1 inch ball of tan clay
½ inch ball of tan clay
three ½ inch balls of brown clay
three ¼ inch balls of orange clay
½ inch ball of white clay
yellow & black clay for eyes
Tools: paperclip

Directions:

1. Owl body: Roll a 1 inch ball and a ½ inch ball of tan clay. Roll three ½ inch balls of brown clay. Roll the 1 inch ball into a fat coil, and form into an egg shape. Place the clay vertically on your work surface resting on the larger end.

2. Wings: Roll two of the brown balls into cone shapes, and flatten slightly to form the wings. Position the wings on opposite sides of the body as shown; press firmly to attach.

3. Head feathers: Flatten the remaining brown ball of clay, and pinch into a triangle shape. Position on top of the head, press gently to attach. Roll the small tan ball of clay into a slight coil.

4. Tail: Attach tan coil to the back of the owl body at the base. Press firmly to attach.

5. Feet and Beak: Roll three ¼ inch balls of orange clay. Position the two of the balls under the owl's body and press to attach. Roll remaining ball into a cone shape to use for the beak.

6. Use the rounded end of the paperclip to create feather texture on the body, the wings and the head feathers. Use the side of the paperclip to add detail lines to the feet and tail.

7. Eyes: Roll two small balls of white clay the same size. Roll two smaller balls of yellow clay, and two smallest balls of black clay for pupils. Position white balls next to each other on the face and press gently to attach. Add circles for yellow eye balls and black pupils. Press to attach.

8. Position the orange cone in between the white circles and press to attach. Use the paperclip to make two nostril holes.

Ask an adult to bake your finished project on a wax paper lined cookie sheet according to clay manufacturer instructions on the package.

1

2

3

4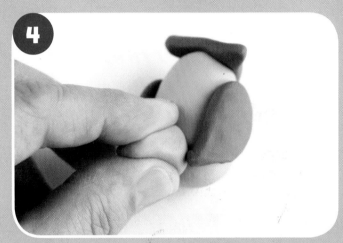

5

6

7

8

Pretty Kitty
Difficulty Level: ★ ★

Materials

1 inch ball of blue clay
two ¾ inch balls of blue clay
three ½ inch balls of blue clay
two ½ inch ball of light blue clay
¼ inch ball of pink clay
white & black clay for eyes

Tools: paperclip, clay tool, chopstick

1

¾

½

¼

Directions:

1. Divide the clay and roll the 1 inch ball of blue clay for the body into an egg shape. Roll a cone from one of the ¾ inch balls of blue clay for the tail, and roll balls for the rest of the body parts.

2. Position the ¾ inch ball of blue clay for the head on the smaller end of the egg shape, and press firmly to attach. Add two ½ inch balls of blue clay for the front feet under the body. Press feet firmly to body to attach.

3. Add the cone for the tail; attach at the bottom, and wrap around side of the body. Divide the remaining ½ inch ball of blue clay in half and roll two small cones for ears. Attach to the top of the head. Pinch each ear to make it pointy.

4. Flatten one of the light blue balls of clay and tap edge of the circle on the table to flatten. Position on chest, with flat side under chin and press to attach. Cut off end of tail with your clay tool and replace with light blue cone.

5. Use the paperclip to add fur texture on the entire kitty by making short strokes through the clay. Keep the marks going in one direction to give it a furry look.

6. Use a chopstick to indent and make a hole in each ear. Add a small cone of pink to the inside of each ear, use chopstick to press pink clay in place.

7. Make the mouth by pressing the rounded end of the paper clip into the clay to form two "U" shapes next to each other.

8. Add a triangle of pink clay to make the nose. Add eyes by making two small balls of white clay and two smaller balls of black clay, and press gently to attach. Add three dots in each "U" shape using the open end of the paperclip. Add whiskers and toe details using the flat side of the paperclip.

Ask an adult to bake your finished project on a wax paper lined cookie sheet according to clay manufacturer instructions on the package.

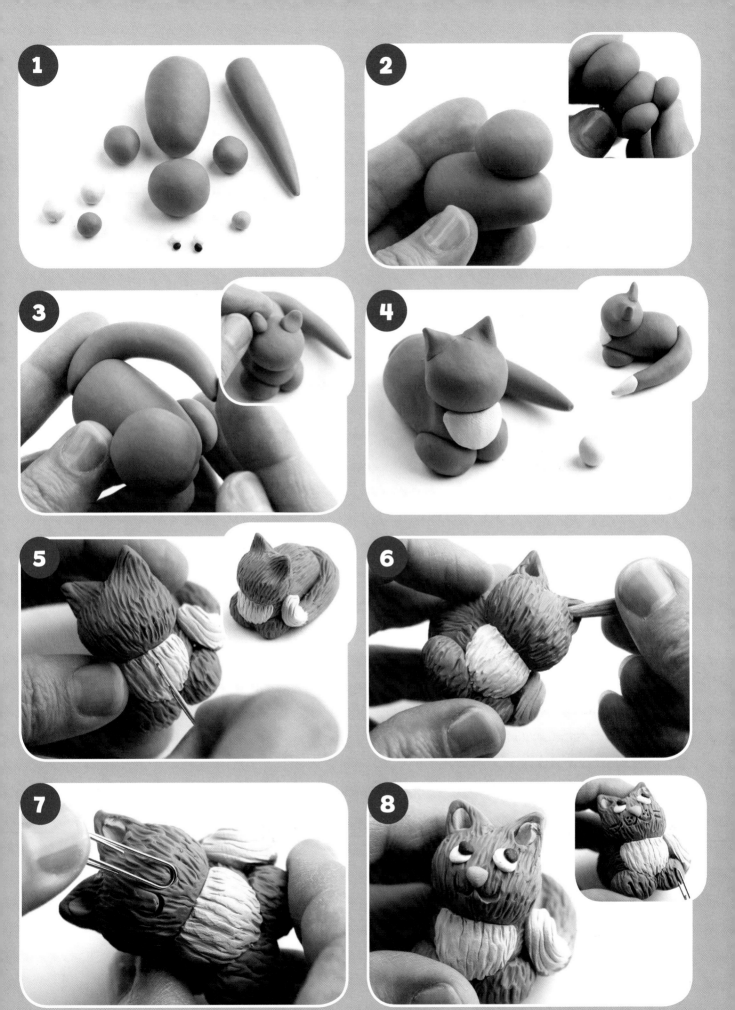

Sweet Puppy

Difficulty Level: ★ ★

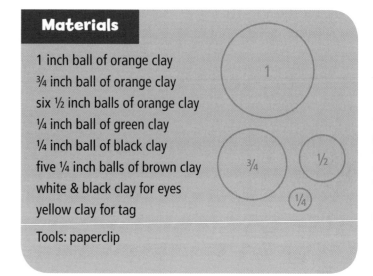

Materials

1 inch ball of orange clay
¾ inch ball of orange clay
six ½ inch balls of orange clay
¼ inch ball of green clay
¼ inch ball of black clay
five ¼ inch balls of brown clay
white & black clay for eyes
yellow clay for tag

Tools: paperclip

Directions:

1. Roll the 1 inch ball of orange clay into a coil for the puppy's body. Use the ¾ inch ball of orange clay to make an egg shape for the head. Take four ½ inch balls of orange clay and roll them into short coils for the legs. Roll one ½ inch ball of orange clay into a cone shape for the tail.

2. Position the head on one end of the body, and press to attach. Add the tail to the other end of the body, and press to secure.

3. Position the four balls under the short fat coil as shown, and press firmly to attach.

4. Divide the last ½ inch ball of orange clay in half and roll two long cones for the ears. Roll a thin green coil for the collar.

5. Position a the green coil around the neck of the puppy. Press gently to attach. Flatten the ears slightly and add on each side of the head pressing gently.

6. Add smile for mouth using the curved end of the paperclip. Press paperclip into the feet to make two lines in each paw.

7. Add small white balls and black pupils for eyes. Add a small black ball for the nose. Add a tiny ball of yellow clay for the tag on the collar.

8. Flatten the five ¼ inch balls of brown clay, and add them as spots to the body of the puppy.

Ask an adult to bake your finished project on a wax paper lined cookie sheet according to clay manufacturer instructions on the package.

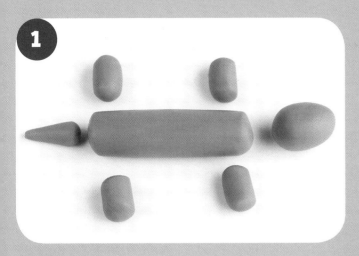

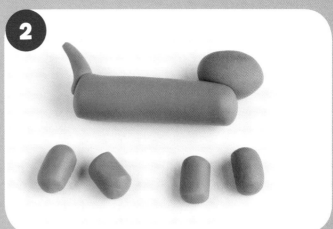

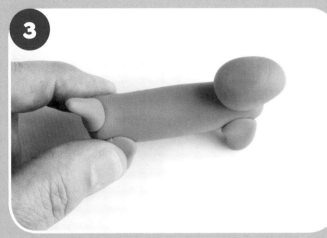

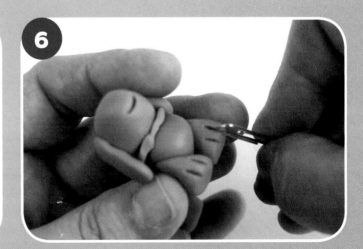

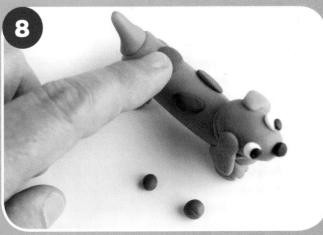

Friendly Fox

Difficulty Level: ★ ★ ★

Materials

1½ inch ball of orange clay for body cone
1 inch ball of orange clay for tail cone
four ¾ inch balls of orange clay
two ½ inch balls of white clay
three ¼ inch balls to form cones of orange clay
white & black clay for eyes and nose

Tools: paperclip, clay tool, chopstick

Directions:

1. Roll clay into shapes and sizes shown. Roll a 1½ inch ball of orange clay to make the cone for the body of the fox. Roll a 1 inch ball of orange clay into a cone for the tail. Use four ¾ inch balls of orange clay for the legs. Make three ¼ inch balls of orange clay and form into cones for ears and the hair on head. Roll two ½ inch balls of white clay for fur details. Use small balls of white and black clay for eyes and nose.

2. To create a cone shape, first roll a thick coil, then continue rolling with your hand on half of the coil. The end will start to thin out and become pointed. Continue rolling until the body is about 4 inches long.

3. Position the clay with the wider end on the bottom, and fold the clay over to make the head. Roll the four ¾ inch balls of orange clay into four short coils. For the two back legs create a pear shape by rolling in the middle of the coil.

4. Position back legs on opposite sides of the bottom, with the wide end toward the back, to support the fox in a sitting position. Press legs firmly toward the body to attach.

5. Flatten one of the balls of white clay, and place on the chest of the fox and press to attach. Take the remaining two leg coils, and position them in front of the chest; press firmly to the body.

6. Use the cone for the tail, cut off the tip and roll a cone of white clay.

7. Replace the tip of the tail with the white cone of clay. Roll tail on table to make it a smooth join. Attach the tail to the bottom of the fox.

8. Add two small cones for the ears and the third orange cone for hair between the ears. (Continued on page 54.)

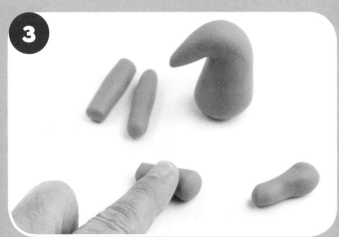

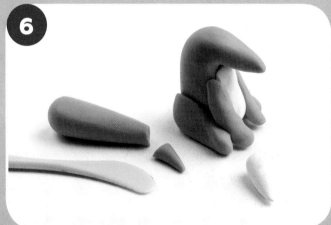

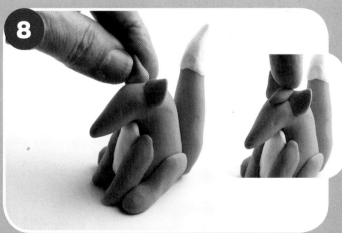

Directions continued:

9. Use the paper clip to add fur texture on the entire fox by making short strokes with the paperclip through the clay. Keep the marks going in one direction to give it a furry look.

10. Make the mouth by dragging the end of the paper clip upward across both sides of the face to form smile. Add a short line to end of the smile line. Use a ball of black clay to make a pointy nose.

11. Add eyes by making two small balls of white clay and two smaller balls of black clay to form each eye; press gently to attach.

12. Put three very small black dots on each side of the nose using the point of the paperclip.

13. Use a chopstick to indent and make a hole in each ear.

14. Add two deeper lines to each foot to form the paws.

Ask an adult to bake your finished project on a wax paper lined cookie sheet according to clay manufacturer instructions on the package.

Alligator

Difficulty Level: ★ ★ ★

Materials

1½ inch ball of green clay
five ¾ inch balls of green clay
two ½ inch balls of green clay
two ¼ inch balls of green clay
½ inch ball of white clay
¼ inch ball of pink clay
white & black clay for eyes

Tools: paperclip, clay tool and foil

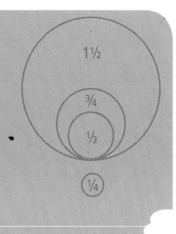

Directions:

1. To make the alligator body, roll a 1½ inch ball of green clay then form it into a cone about six inches long. Roll five ¾ inch balls of green clay, turn one of the balls into a coil the same length as the alligator for the back ridge. Make two ½ inch balls, and two ¼ inch balls of green clay. Take a ½ inch ball of white clay and roll a thin coil for the teeth. Make a ¼ inch ball of pink clay and roll it into a coil for the tongue. You will also need white and black clay for the eyes.

2. Take the four ¾ inch balls of green clay, and then roll each one into a short coil. Line up the feet facing forward on opposite sides of the body.

3. Position the feet under the body as shown. Press feet firmly toward body to attach. Flatten the front of the feet with your thumb.

4. Start the back ridge coil about an inch in from the end of the coil. Press gently to attach the coil down the middle of the back. Cut off any extra coil at the end of the tail.

5. Use the clay tool to slice halfway through larger end of the coil to form an open mouth. Smooth the mouth with your fingers.

6. Add a pink tongue in the middle of the bottom jaw.

7. Divide the coil of white clay in half. Position the coils to follow the edge of the upper and lower jaw. Press coil gently to attach, and cut off extra clay.

8. Press the paperclip into the white coil to make teeth. (Continued on page 58.)

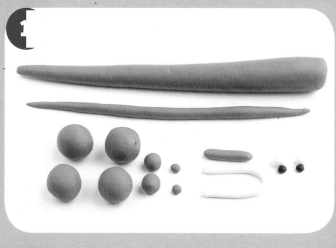

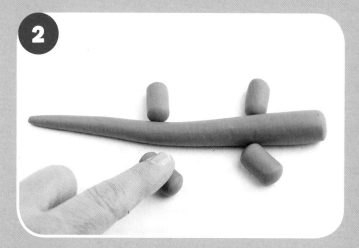

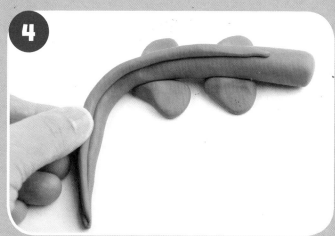

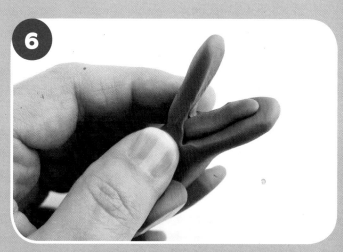

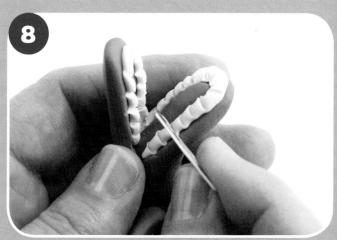

Directions Continued:

9. Press the flat edge of the paperclip into the coil all the way down the back.

10. Use a paper clip to add detail lines to the feet.

11. Add horizontal and vertical detail lines to the alligator's body and lines across the nose using the side of the paperclip.

12. Pinch each section of the back ridge to make it stand up.

13. Place two ½ inch balls of green clay side by side at the end of the back ridge. Add eyes by making two small balls of white clay and two smaller balls of black clay to form each eye. Position on the head as shown, and press gently to attach.

14. Add two small balls of green clay to the end of the nose to form nostrils; make a hole in each using the open end of the paperclip.

15. Add a line down the middle of the tongue.

16. Position the body and the tail to give the alligator some character.

    Support the raised tail and head with foil while baking to keep it from sagging.

Ask an adult to bake your finished project on a wax paper lined cookie sheet according to clay manufacturer instructions on the package.

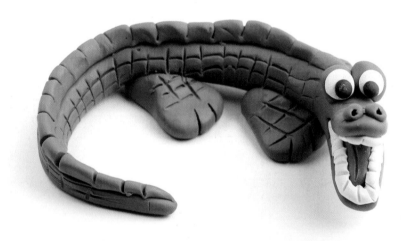

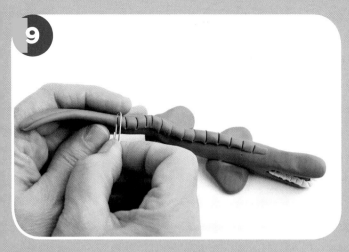

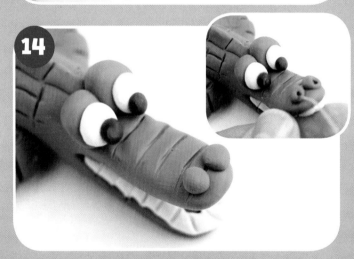

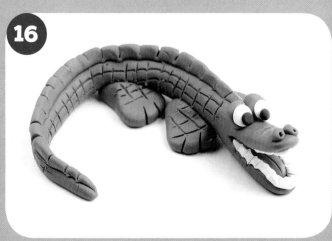

It's "Magic" Color Clay

Unless you started with this section, you will have a lot of small bits of clay in different colors left over by now. What will you do with all of this "mixed up" clay? Don't worry. This is a special opportunity to let the clay make some MAGIC for you; see how the projects that follow become unique one-of-a-kind masterpieces using "Magic" color clay!

Happy Heart
Difficulty Level: ★

Materials

(½) 2 oz. brick of red clay
1 inch ball of "Magic" color clay
¼ inch ball of pink clay
blue clay & black clay for eyes
Tools: straw; roller

Directions:

1. Use a roller to flatten red clay for the heart. Cut out the heart shape using the template on this page. Keep scraps.

2. Gather some of your clay fragments, and roll a ball 1 inch in diameter. Make sure the clay is not pulling apart or crumbling. If it is, continue to roll it in your hands until it is smooth and has no cracks. Roll the clay into a long coil. To form the twisted colors, hold one end of the coil in place and gently roll the other end away from you to cause the coil to form spirals of color.

3. Start at the point of the heart and begin wrapping the spiral colored coil around the entire edge. Press gently against the edge of the heart as you wrap to attach. Cut off the extra coil, press ends together.

4. Roll two equal size blue balls of clay for the eyes; position them, and press gently to attach to the heart. Add smaller black balls of clay for the pupils.

5. Roll a small, thin pink coil for the mouth, form into a smile, position, and press gently to attach to the heart.

6. Use a straw to punch a hole for hanging your heart.

Ask an adult to bake your finished project on a wax paper lined cookie sheet according to clay manufacturer instructions on the package.

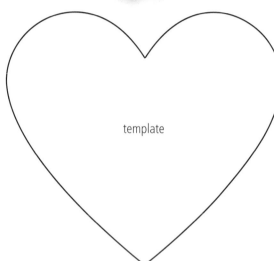

template

Hearts Galore!

"Magic" Color Clay makes each heart one of a kind!

Make a bunch and share the love with your family and friends!

Snazzy Snail

Difficulty Level: ★

Materials

(½) 2 oz. brick of yellow clay
1 inch ball of "Magic" color clay
white clay & black clay for eyes
Tools: paperclip

Directions:

1. Roll half of the yellow clay into a cone about 3 inches long to form the snail's body.

2. Roll the remaining yellow clay into a ball. Place ball in the middle of the snail's body.

3. Gather some mixed up "Magic" color clay for the shell, and roll a ball 1 inch in diameter. Roll it in your hands until the surface of the ball is smooth and has no cracks. Roll the clay into a long coil. To form the twisted colors, hold one end of the coil in place and gently roll the other end away from you to cause the coil to form spirals of color.

4. Begin wrapping the spiral colored coil around the entire base of the ball. Continue wrapping the coil around the ball directly on top of the previous row. Press gently as you wrap to attach.

5. Cut off extra coil at the top of the shell, and curl the end of coil into the middle.

6. Roll two white balls of clay for the eyes, position them, and press gently to attach. Add smaller black balls of clay for the pupils, and press gently to attach.

7. Use the rounded end of the paperclip to indent a smiling mouth. Make two nostril holes with the open end of the paperclip.

8. Position the head and the tail to give your snail some character.

   Ask an adult to bake your finished project on a wax paper lined cookie sheet according to clay manufacturer instructions on the package.

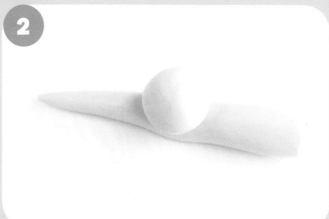

Chameleon

Difficulty Level: ★

Materials

1 inch ball of "Magic" color clay
¾ inch ball of "Magic" color clay
½ inch ball of yellow clay
red clay & black clay
Tools: paperclip, clay tool to cut

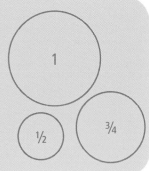

Directions:

1. Gather enough mixed up "Magic" color clay to make two balls; 1 inch and ¾ inch in diameter. Roll each ball in your hands until the surface is smooth and has no cracks. Roll the larger ball of clay into a long thick coil for the body. To form the twisted colors, hold one end of the coil in place and gently roll the other end away from you to cause the coil to form spirals of color. Roll the coil on one half, the end will start to thin out and become pointed. Continue rolling until it is about 5 inches long.

2. Cut off the thicker end of coil with a clay tool. Round the end of the coil with your fingers to form the head.

3. Roll the thin end of coil into a spiral shape to form tail. Take the ¾ inch ball of "Magic" color clay, and roll into a coil. Follow directions in step one to form spiral colors. Cut off four 1 inch length pieces for the legs. Set the remaining coil aside.

4. Position the feet under the body. Press feet firmly toward the body to attach. Roll the end of the coils under to form end of feet.

5. Use the leftover coil of "Magic" color clay to make a coil down the middle of the back to form the back ridge. Cut off the extra coil part way down the tail. Press coil gently to attach to body.

6. Use the side of the paperclip to make ridge marks the length of the coil.

7. Add eyes by making two equal size balls of yellow clay and two smaller balls of black clay to form each eye. Position on the head, and press gently to attach. The eyes should be looking in different directions. Make mouth with end of paperclip.

8. Add toe marks using the side of the paperclip. Add a red tongue coming out of the mouth. Position the chameleon to give it character.

    Ask an adult to bake your finished project on a wax paper lined cookie sheet according to clay manufacturer instructions on the package.

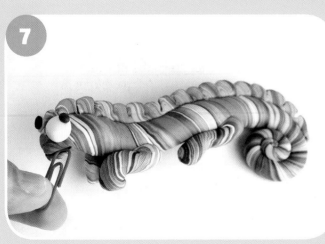

Dancing Polar Bear

Difficulty Level: ★ ★

Materials

2 oz. brick of white clay
½ inch ball of blue clay
½ inch ball of "Magic" color clay
black clay for eyes and nose
Tools: paperclip, pencil with eraser

½

¼

Directions:

1. Divide the clay: Start with a 2 ounce brick of white clay. Divide the clay in half on the lines, and roll a large fat coil for the body. Divide the remaining clay on the line. Take one of the pieces and remove two ¼ inch balls for ears, and two smaller balls for eyes, then roll the rest into a ball for the head. Divide the last piece of clay into four equal parts for the legs; roll them into four short fat coils.

2. Body: Roll the large ball into a short, fat coil to form the body of the bear. Place on a piece of wax paper, and flatten slightly with your palm. Roll the ball for the head into a slight cone shape. Position the head overlapping one end of the body, and press to flatten and attach.

3. Legs: Position the legs so that the bear looks as though it is dancing, with two legs under and two over the body to give the bear more dimension. Press each leg firmly onto the body to attach.

4. Feet: Use the paperclip to add toe detail by pressing it into the clay.

5. Face: Add two small white balls for eyes; press gently to secure. Add two smaller black balls for the pupils, and press gently. Add a ball of black clay for the nose. Use the open end of the paperclip to form the mouth, and to add three freckles to the side of the nose.

6. Ears: Flatten the ears slightly; use a pencil eraser to indent the middle of each ear. Press each finished ear onto the top of the head.

7. Scarf: Gather enough mixed up "Magic" color clay to roll a ½ inch ball. Roll the clay in your hands until the surface of the ball is smooth and has no cracks. Roll the clay into a long coil. To form the twisted colors, hold one end of the coil in place and gently roll the other end away from you to cause the coil to form spirals of color. Drape the coil around the neck and down the side of the bear. Press to flatten the scarf and secure in place. Cut off extra clay.

8. Hat: Use a solid color clay that matches your "Magic" color clay coil to make the hat. Roll the clay into a fat coil. Position on head and press to attach. Put a spiral of "Magic" color clay coil at the end of the hat for a pom-pom. Add a small coil of "Magic" color clay above the eyes to form the brim of the hat.

Ask an adult to bake your finished project on a wax paper lined cookie sheet according to clay manufacturer instructions on the package.

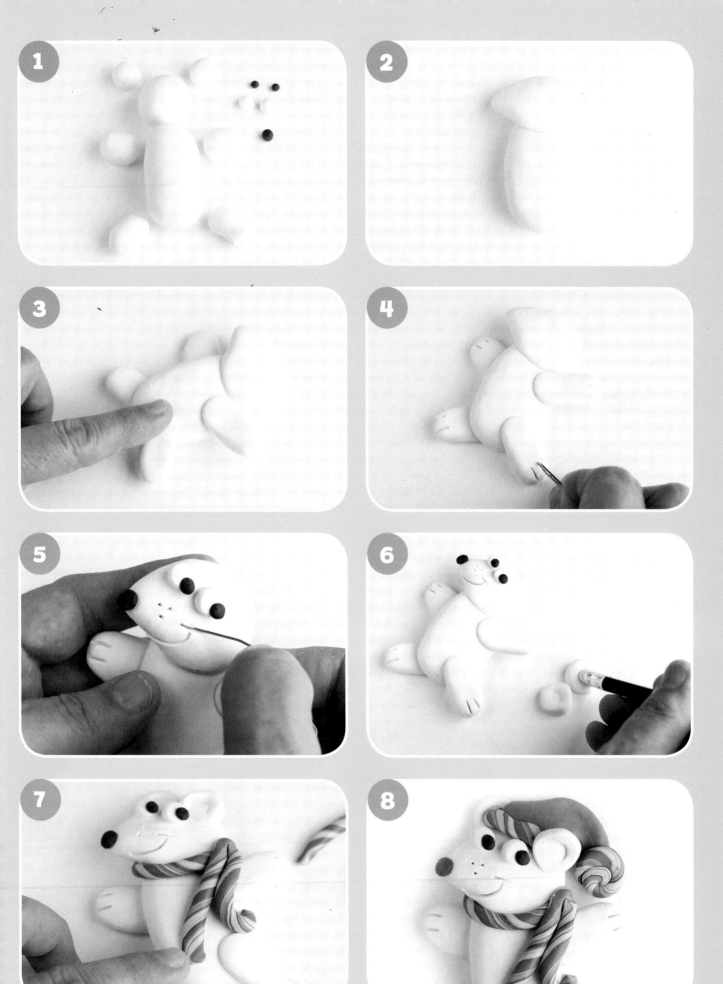

Turtle

Difficulty Level: ★ ★

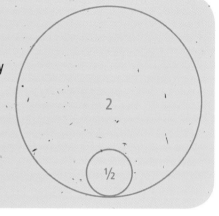

Directions:

1. Make a ½ inch ball of the blue clay and set it aside for the tail. Divide the rest of the blue clay into three equal pieces. Roll two pieces into coils about 3 inches long for the legs. To make the head, roll the last piece of blue into a cone.

2. Position two coils across each other at right angles to form legs, and press firmly in the middle to attach.

3. Add the head, position it on the legs, and press the neck end firmly to attach. Take the clay set aside for the tail and roll it into a cone. Position and attach the tail by pressing gently.

4. To form a support for the shell, use a ball of foil about 1½ inch in diameter. Roll a slab of any color clay and wrap it around the foil ball. Place the clay wrapped foil ball in the middle of the four legs, and press firmly to attach.

5. Gather enough mixed up "Magic" color clay to roll a 2-inch ball. Roll the clay in your hands until the surface of the ball is smooth and has no cracks. Flatten the ball with a roller to make a multicolored slab. Drape the clay over the ball on the turtle to form the shell, and press gently in the middle to attach. Drape over the feet, head, and tail. Be sure the feet, head, and tail are all visible. Trim clay if needed.

6. Roll a coil with enough mixed up "Magic" color clay to go around the lower edge of the shell. To form the twisted colors, hold one end of the coil in place and gently roll the other end away from you to cause the coil to form spirals of color. Position around the edge of the shell, and press to attach. Cut off extra clay coil.

7. Add some spirals to the shell using "Magic" color clay coils. Spiral colors to form circles, and press gently to attach to shell.

8. Add two small white balls for eyes, and press gently to secure. Add two small black balls for the pupils of the eyes, and press in place. Use the rounded end of the paperclip to form each side of the mouth. Add two lines to each foot by using the side of the paperclip. Use the open end of the paper clip to make two nostril holes.

Support the head with a ball of foil while baking.

Ask an adult to bake your finished project on a wax paper lined cookie sheet according to clay manufacturer instructions on the package.

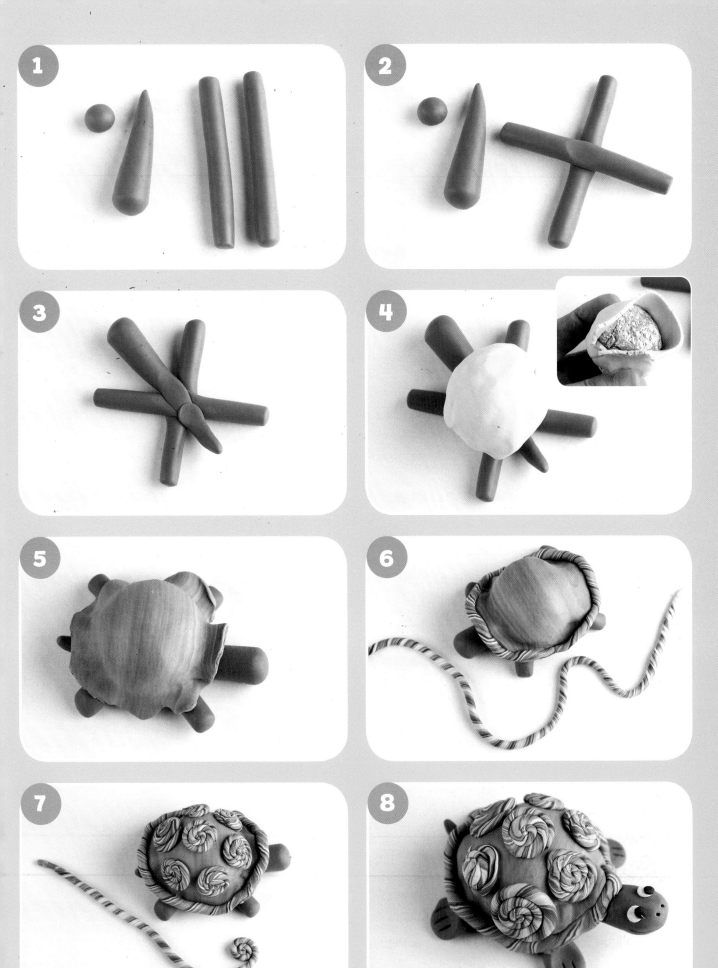

Trinket Box
Difficulty Level: ★ ★

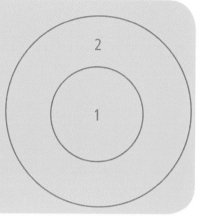

Materials

(½) 2 oz. brick of yellow clay
2 inch ball of "Magic" color clay
1 inch ball of "Magic" color clay
Tools: roller, clay tool, paper, pencil, scissors

Directions:

1. Choose a color clay you like and roll out enough clay to make a circle ¼" thick. Trace the template below; cut out the circle with scissors, place circle on the clay, and cut clay. This clay circle will be the base of the box.

2. Gather enough mixed up "Magic" color clay to make a 1-inch and a 2-inch ball. Roll the clay in your hands until the surface of the ball is smooth and has no cracks. Roll the clay into long coils. To form the twisted colors, hold one end of the coil in place and gently roll the other end away from you to cause the coil to form spiral colors. Move your hands down the coil and repeat process until the whole coil has spirals of color.

3. Use the longer coil; place a clay circle on wax paper to form the base. Position the coil around the edge of the circle and press coil firmly to the edge of the circle.

4. Continue placing the second layer of coil directly on top of the previous layer, and press gently down to secure coils together. Repeat this process around the shape to make the box seven rows high. Cut off extra coil. Press end of coil to secure.

5. To make the lid, start the coil in the center of the template and spiral the coil around until it is the slightly larger than the template. Making the coil larger than the template will keep it from falling into the box. Cut off the extra coil.

6. Add a small coil about a ¼ inch inside the edge of the lid. This will keep the lid from sliding off the box after it is baked.

7. Add a small rolled up coil to the other side of the lid middle to make the box handle.

8. Try the lid on the box to make sure it fits.

   Bake the lid and the box separately; not as a closed box. The box and lid will stick together if stacked while baking, and it will be hard to get them apart without breaking.

   Ask an adult to bake your finished project on a wax paper lined cookie sheet according to clay manufacturer instructions on the package.

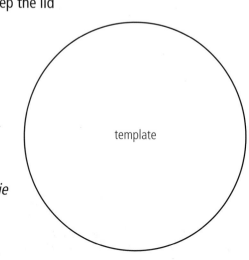

template

Dinosaur Pencil Buddy
Difficulty Level: ★ ★

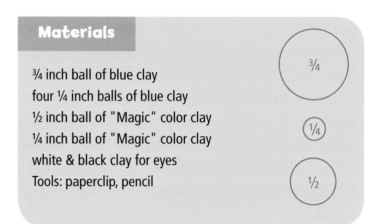

Materials

¾ inch ball of blue clay
four ¼ inch balls of blue clay
½ inch ball of "Magic" color clay
¼ inch ball of "Magic" color clay
white & black clay for eyes
Tools: paperclip, pencil

¾

¼

½

Directions:

1. Dinosaur body: Roll a ¾ inch ball of blue clay, and four ¼ inch balls of blue clay. Roll the large ball into a cone. To create this shape, first start by making a thick coil; then continue to roll it with your finger on half of the coil. The end will start to thin out and become pointed. Continue rolling until the body is about 2 inches long.

2. Curve the cone to form the head, body and tail. Flatten a ¼ inch piece of the "Magic" color clay, and press onto the belly of the dinosaur.

3. Feet: Roll the ¼ inch balls of blue clay in one direction to make short coils. Position them on the body, and press gently to attach.

4. Back ridge: Roll the ½ inch ball of "Magic" color clay into a twisted coil slightly shorter than the length of the dinosaur body. Attach the coil down the middle of the back. Pinch off extra coil of clay at the end of the tail. Press gently to attach coil.

5. Use the flat side of the paperclip to create details on the back ridge.

6. Use the opened end of the paperclip to make a smiling mouth. Add details using the paperclip, and make horizontal lines across the chest.

7. Add eyes by making two small balls of white clay and two smaller balls of black clay to form each eye. Position them on the head, and press gently to attach.

8. Add nostril holes with the open end of the paperclip. Use the edge of the paperclip to add lines for the toes.

   Before baking, use the pointed end of a pencil to form an opening in the base of the dinosaur, and fit the eraser end into the hole. Remove pencil before baking.

   Ask an adult to bake your finished project on a wax paper lined cookie sheet according to clay manufacturer instructions on the package.

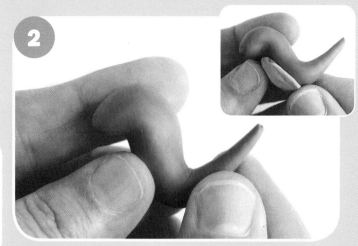

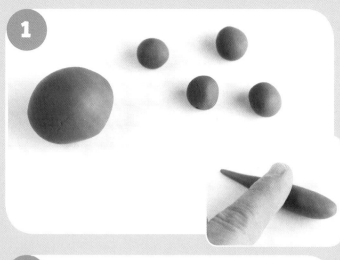

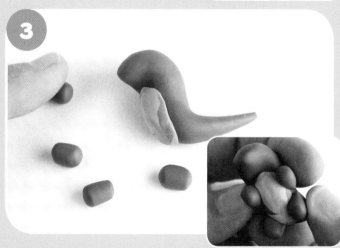

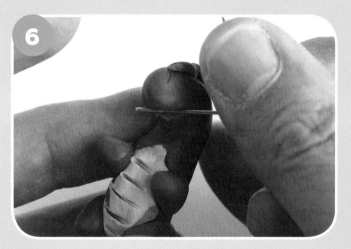

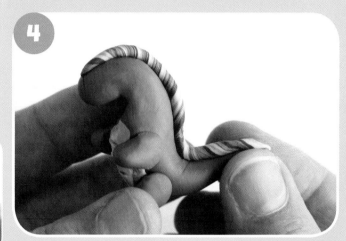

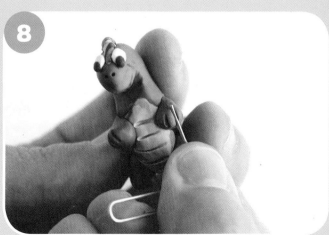

Rainbow Hedgehog
Difficulty Level: ★

Materials

1 inch ball of brown clay
4 ½ inch balls of brown color clay
3 ¼ inch balls of brown clay
1 inch ball of "Magic" color clay
white & black clay for eyes; and nose
Tools: roller, paperclip, clay tool, pencil

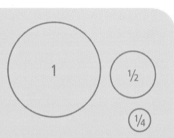

Directions:

1. Divide the clay and roll all balls of clay needed for project.

2. Roll the 1 inch brown ball into a cone. Add the legs to each side of the body, and press firmly to attach.

3. Roll the "Magic" color clay in your hands until the surface of the ball is smooth and has no cracks. Flatten the ball with a roller to form a multicolored; flattened circle, roll to ¼ inch thickness.

4. Drape around the face and over the back of the hedgehog, do not cover the feet or tail, and press gently to attach. Trim clay as necessary. Save extra clay for another project.

5. Use the edge of the paperclip to add texture to the back. Add two toe lines on each foot using the paperclip.

6. Use the eraser end of a pencil to indent the middle of the ears. Place finished ears on head, and press gently to attach. Roll a small cone for the tail, and attach to rear of hedgehog.

7. Add eyes by making two small balls of white clay and two smaller balls of black clay to form each eye, and press gently to attach. Add a small ball of black clay to make the nose.

8. Make the mouth by rolling the end of the paperclip upward across both sides of the face to form a smile. Add short lines to the ends of smile line. Add three dots to each side of the nose with the end of the paperclip.

Ask an adult to bake your finished project on a wax paper lined cookie sheet according to clay manufacturer instructions on the package.

Funky Frame

Difficulty Level: ★ ★

Directions:

1. Gather enough mixed up "Magic" color clay to roll a 2-inch ball. Roll the clay in your hands until the surface of the ball is smooth and has no cracks. Place the Magic color clay on wax paper, and flatten the clay with a roller until it is the thickness of a piece of cardboard.

2. Using a clay tool, and a wooden craft stick, cut a rectangle. Set aside extra clay to use for coils.

3. Line up the wooden craft stick with the edge of the frame and use your clay tool to cut a rectangular opening. Remove extra clay in the middle of the frame.

4. Use the extra clay trimmed off the frame to roll coils. To create the twisted colors, first roll a coil, hold one end of the coil in place, and gently roll the other end away from you to form spirals of color. Line the inside and outside edge of frame with a "Magic" color clay twisted coil. Press gently in place.

5. Place black clay on wax paper, and flatten the clay with a roller until it is the thickness of a piece of cardboard. Carefully trace around the edge of the frame. Use the clay tool to cut the black clay to be slightly smaller than the frame. Collect the trimmed off black clay to use for stand.

6. Roll trimmed off black clay into a cone. Flatten the bottom of the cone by tapping it on the table a few times.

7. Attach the cone to the black rectangle; put it in the middle of the long edge for horizontal frame or in the middle of the short edge for a vertical frame.

8. Line up the front and the back of the frame to make sure it fits together.

Bake the black stand flat with the cone facing up. Keep the two sides of the frame apart while you bake them. When the parts of the frame have cooled, add a favorite picture and glue the frame together with craft glue.

Ask an adult to bake your finished project on a wax paper lined cookie sheet according to clay manufacturer instructions on the package.

Love it!
Make a heart-shaped frame.
Use a cookie cutter to make it easy!

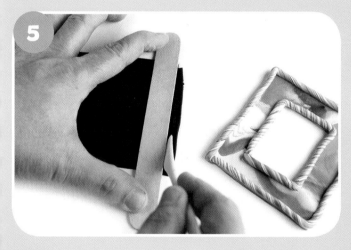

Acknowledgments:

I would like to dedicate this book to my loving family, and to all my students over the years who have inspired me to create these fun projects.

A special thank you to my good friends John Paul Endress and Janet Skiles for all their help and encouragement.

I hope that this book will bring you some fun and inspire your family to spend some time creating together.

From my heart to yours!

TT

Table of Contents

Bibliographical Note

Clay Play! 24 Whimsical Projects is a new work, first
published by Dover Publications, Inc., in 2014.

International Standard Book Number
ISBN-13: 978-0-486-77984-3
ISBN-10: 0-486-77984-X

Manufactured in the United States by Courier Corporation
77984X01   2014
www.doverpublications.com

CLAY PLAY!

24 Whimsical Projects

by
Terry Taylor

Dover Publications, Inc.
Mineola, New York